# Fabric
# Jewellery

SEARCH PRESS

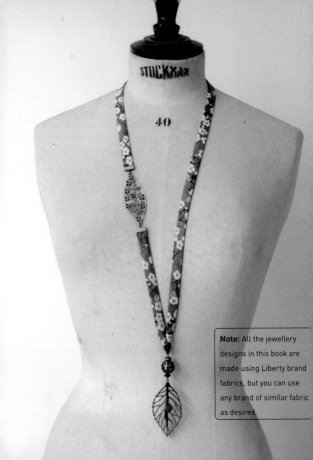

**Note:** All the jewellery designs in this book are made using Liberty brand fabrics, but you can use any brand of similar fabric as desired.

# Contents

**Materials** 7

**Basic techniques** 10

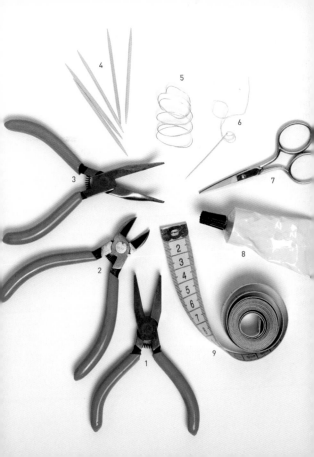

# Materials

## Tools

**Flat-nosed pliers (1)** are used for picking up and holding small pieces, but also for bending metal wire and squeezing closed clamps or crimp beads.

**Wire cutters (2)** are used for cutting chains and wire.

**Round-nosed pliers (3)** are used for picking up, twisting and shaping small metal items.

**Toothpicks (4)** are very handy for carrying out delicate tasks – for example, applying spots of glue to the inside of findings.

**Wire (5)** Gives form to soft material such as fabric, and holds it in shape.

**Needle and thread (6)** are used for any small sewing jobs.

**Sewing scissors (7)** are invaluable for cutting fabric, thread and cords.

**Glue (8)** Transparent, slow-drying glue is generally used. A special textile glue can be used for sticking fabric to fabric.

**Tape measure (9)** Indispensable for measuring lengths of fabric or chain.

## Jewellery findings

**Large ribbon clamps (1)** 3cm (1¼in) wide.

**Classic ribbon clamps (2)** 12mm (½in) wide.

**Square cord ends (3)** 6mm (¼in) in diameter.

**Large cord ends (4)** 5mm (¼in) in diameter.

**Medium cord ends (5)** 3mm (⅛in) in diameter.

**Small cord ends (6)** 2mm (¹⁄₁₆in) in diameter.

**Ball chain ends (7)**

**Large jump rings (8)** 8 × 10mm (⁵⁄₁₆ x ½in).

**Jump rings (9)** 4 × 6mm (⅛ x ¼in).

**Round jump rings (10)** 4mm (¼in) in diameter.

**Snap clasp (11)**

**Lobster clasps (12)**

**Ball chain clasps (13)**

**Eye pins (14)**

**Light curb chain (15)**

**Ball chain (16)**

**Double chain (17)**

**Snake chain (18)**

**Fine trace chain (19)**

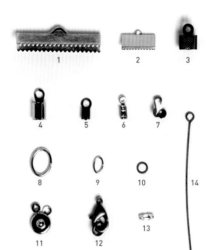

1

2

3

4

5

6

7

8

9

10

14

11

12

13

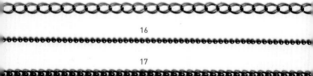

15

16

17

18

19

# Basic techniques

**Attaching pieces together using a jump ring:** Using flat-nosed and round-nosed pliers, twist open the jump ring (rather than pulling it apart).

**Forming an eye loop:** Cut the metal pin approximately 1cm (½in) above the point where the eye loop will be positioned, and twist the pin to an angle of about 45 degrees. Shape the pin around the round-nosed pliers to form an eye loop.

**Inserting bias binding into a ribbon clamp:** Put a dab of glue inside the ribbon clamp and insert the end of the bias binding. Use the flat-nosed pliers to close and press the clamp together around the bias binding.

**Inserting the end of a cord into a cord end:** Put a dab of glue inside the cord end and insert the end of the cord. Close and squeeze down on one of the sides with the flat-nosed pliers, then squeeze the second side of the cord end on to the first.

# Necklace

**Materials:** 48cm (19in) of 'Phoebe A' pink Liberty bias binding; 30cm (11¾in) fine trace chain; 11 small beads to match the bias binding; 1 small leaf charm; 2 ribbon clamps; 3 jump rings; 5 metal pins

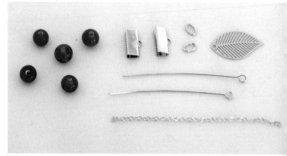

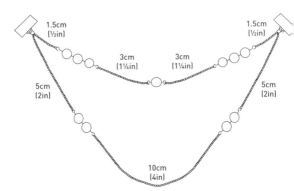

**1** Insert the ends of the bias binding into the ribbon clamps. Attach jump rings to each of the ribbon clamps. Cut the chain into two lengths measuring 1.5cm (½in), two lengths measuring 3cm (1¼in), two lengths measuring 5cm (2in) and one length measuring 10cm (4in).

**2** Thread three beads on to a metal pin and make an eye loop at each end of the beads. Continue until you have made two sets of three beads on met pins, two sets of two beads and a single bead.

**3** Attach one of the jump rings to a 1.5cm (½in) length of chain, followed by a set of three beads. Then attach a 3cm (1¼in) length of chain, the single bead, the second 3cm (1¼in) length of chain, the other set of three beads and finally the second 1.5cm (½in) length of chain.

**4** Attach the free end of this last length of chain to the jump ring on the second ribbon clamp.

**5** In the same way, attach a 5cm (2in) length of chain to one of the lower jump rings, followed by a set of two beads, the 10cm (4in) length of chain, the second set of two beads and finally the remaining 5cm (2in) length of chain. Attach the free end of this last length of chain to the lower jump ring on the second ribbon clamp.

**6** Using a jump ring, attach the leaf charm to the 10cm (4in) length of chain.

# Matching bracelets

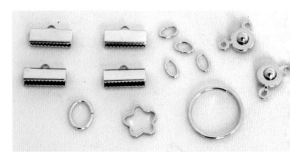

Here are some delightful, easy-to-make bracelets each in its own style. Wear them on their own or together.

## Making the ring bracelet

Materials for a 17cm (6¾in) ring bracelet: 2 × 'Adelajda D' blue Liberty bias binding, 12.5cm (5in) in length; 1 small star charm; 1 snap clasp; 2 ribbon clamps; 1 ring, 16mm (½in) in diameter; 3 jump rings

1 Pass a piece of bias binding through the ring and fold it in half around the ring so the ends of the binding are one on top of the other.

2 Insert both ends of the bias binding into a ribbon clamp.

3 Repeat steps 1 and 2 with the second piece of bias binding.

4 Attach one half of the clasp to each of the ribbon clamps using a jump ring.

5 Attach the small star charm to one of the jump rings on the clasp using another jump ring.

## Making the charm bracelet

Materials for a 17cm (6¾in) charm bracelet: 15cm (6in) of 'Rania C' blue Liberty bias binding; 1 flower charm; 1 snap clasp; 2 ribbon clamps; 1 large jump ring; 2 jump rings

1 Twist open the large jump ring and attach the flower charm before closing the ring.

2 Pass the bias binding through the large jump ring.

3 Insert each end of the bias binding into a ribbon clamp.

4 Attach one half of the snap clasp to each of the ribbon clamps using a jump ring.

## Making the bow bracelet

Materials for a 17cm (6¾in) bow bracelet: 27cm (10¾in) of 'Melly D' blue Liberty bias binding; 1 snap clasp; 2 ribbon clamps; 2 jump rings

**1** Cut 15cm (6in) of bias binding and insert each end of the binding into a ribbon clamp.

**2** Attach one half of the clasp to each of the ribbon clamps using a jump ring.

**3** Cut 9cm (3½in) of binding. Bring the ends of the strip together to form a ring, overlapping the ends a little, then glue the overlap together.

**4** Glue the bias binding ring in the middle of the bias binding bracelet (gluing the join in the ring to the bracelet).

**5** Flatten the bias binding ring and wrap the remaining 3cm (1¼in) of binding round it to form the bow. Glue the ends into place on to the inside of the bracelet.

# Earrings

Materials: 2 × 'Phoebe L' pink cord, 14cm (5½in) in length; 2 earring hooks; 2 small hollow star charms; 2 coloured star charms to match the cord; 2 hollow star charms; 6 medium cord ends; 2 square cord ends; 6 round jump rings

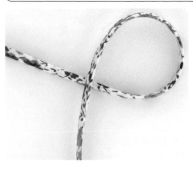

**1** Cut three lengths of cord measuring 4cm (1½in), 4.5cm (1¾in) and 5.5cm (2¼in).

**2** Insert one end of each of the lengths into a cord end.

**3** Attach a small star charm to the eye loop on the cord end on the 4cm (1½in) length using a jump ring. Attach a coloured star charm to the 4.5cm (1¾in) length. Then attach a hollow star charm to the 5.5cm (2¼in) length.

4 Bunch the three free ends of the cords together, laying them partially on top of one another (the cord with the small hollow star first, then the coloured charm, then the large hollow star charm) and insert them into a square cord end.

5 Attach the square cord end directly to the eye loop on the earring mount.

6 Repeat the above steps to make the second earring.

# Spiral bracelets

Materials for a 17cm (6¾in) bracelet: 2 × 'Capel R' pink Liberty cord, 20cm (7¾in) in length and 20cm (7¾in) of 'Mitsi' grey Liberty cord; 3 × wire, 22cm (8¾in) in length; 3 × thick leather lace, 14cm (5½in) in length; 1 snap clasp; 6 large cord ends; 2 large jump rings; 2 jump rings

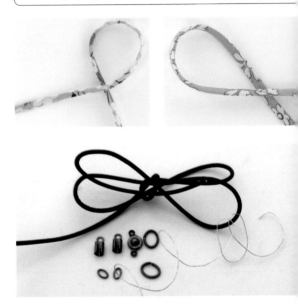

20cm (7¾in)

wire

1 Thread one of the pieces of wire through one of the cords.

rod

2 Wrap the cord around a rod (the handle of a paintbrush or a pencil, for example) to create tight spirals.

cord

3 Remove the rod. Thread a leather lace through the middle of the spiral and pull on both ends of the cord at the same time to expand the spiral out over the full length of the leather lace.

**4** Cut off the ends of wire that are sticking out and insert the two ends of the spiral and the leather lace into the cord ends.

**5** Repeat the above steps to make two other leather laces wrapped in a spiral and finished off with cord ends.

**6** At each end, attach the cord ends of the three leather laces to a large jump ring.

**7** Attach one half of the snap clasp to each of the large jump rings using a jump ring.

# Beaded necklace

**Materials:** 1.3m (51in) of 'Wiltshire L' blue Liberty bias binding; 40cm (15¾in) matching satin bias ribbon; 5 beads around 17mm (¾in) in diameter with a hole at least 5mm (¼in) in diameter (choose a colour that matches the bias binding); 4 beads around 12mm (½in) in diameter (the colour doesn't matter as these beads will be hidden); 2 ribbon clamps; 2 small cord ends; 2 jump rings

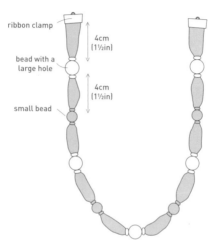

ribbon clamp

4cm
(1½in)

bead with a
large hole

4cm
(1½in)

small bead

**1** Insert one end of the bias binding into a ribbon clamp.

**2** Approximately 4cm (1½in) from the clamp, make two knots, one on top of the other. Pass the bias binding through one of the beads with a large hole and slide the bead up to the knots. Make two more knots, one on top of the other, to hold the bead in place.

3 Approximately 4cm (1½in) from the first bead, make two knots, one on top of the other. Unfold the bias binding and put one of the small beads inside. Wrap the bead in the binding. You can join the bias binding back together with a dab of glue. Make two knots, one on top of the other.

4 Repeat steps 2 and 3 so that you have alternated five visible beads and four hidden beads.

5 Insert the free end of the bias binding into a ribbon clamp.

6 Insert the ends of the satin ribbon into the small cord ends.

7 Attach the ribbon clamps to the small cord ends using a jump ring.

# 36 · Hairband

**Materials:** 3 × 'Wiltshire S' Liberty cord, 50cm (19¾in) in length; 50cm (19¾in) red satin ribbon; 30 to 40cm (11¾ to 15¾in) elastic for hairband (depending on head measurement); 2 ribbon clamps; 1 medium cord end

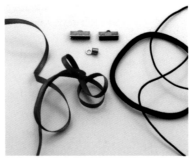

**1** Insert the ends of each of the three pieces of cord and ribbon into a ribbon clamp. The cords must be perfectly aligned, with the cord seams underneath. The satin ribbon is placed on top of the middle cord.

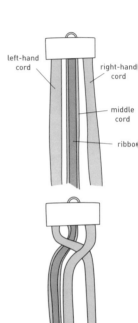

left-hand cord

right-hand cord

middle cord

ribbon

**2** Cross the left-hand cord over the middle cord and the ribbon.

**3** Cross the right-hand cord over the new central cord.

**4** Continue to plait the cords for about 40cm (15¾in). The satin ribbon should always stay positioned on top of the same cord.

**5** Cut off the plaited cords and ribbon at the same length and insert the ends into the second ribbon clamp.

**6** Pass the elastic through the eye loops of the two ribbon clamps, then make a knot at each end.

**7** Cut open the eye loop of the medium cord end using the wire cutters and place the elastic and its two ends, under the knots, in the cord-end cylinder.

**8** Close the medium cord end using the flat-nosed pliers.

# Filigree necklace

Materials: 72cm (28¼in) of floral print bias binding; 1 large filigree piece (at leas
3cm (1¼in) in diameter); 6 small filigree pieces (around 2cm/¾in in diameter);
1 lobster clasp; 16 ribbon clamps; 16 jump rings

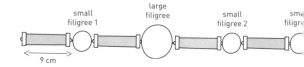

small filigree 1

large filigree

small filigree 2

sm filigre

9 cm

**1** Cut eight pieces of bias binding, around 9cm (3½in) in length.

**2** Insert the ends of each piece of bias binding into ribbon clamps.

**3** Attach the filigree pieces to the ribbon clamps using jump rings.

The large filigree piece is inserted in second place.

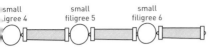

small filigree 4    small filigree 5    small filigree 6

**4** Attach one half of the clasp to each of the end ribbon clamps using a jump ring.

# Chain bracelet

Materials for a 17cm (6¾in) bracelet: 15cm (6in) of 'Glenjade A' dark blue bias binding; 16cm (6¼in) of light curb chain; 1 black skull charm; 1 flat black, disc bead; 1 snap clasp, 2 large cord ends; 4 jump rings; 1 metal pin; 1 crimp bead

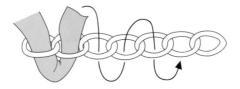

**1** Thread the bias binding through the chain, up through one link and down through the next.

**2** Insert the ends of the bias binding into the large cord ends.

**3** At each end, attach the eye loop of the cord end, the last link of the chain and one half of the snap clasp to a jump ring.

4 Using a jump ring, attach the disc bead to one of the jump rings attached to the clasp.

5 Thread the metal pin through the skull charm and crimp the bead on the end of the pin, under the skull. On the end of the pin above the skull, make an eye loop. Attach the charm to the bracelet by passing a jump ring through the eye loop and through one of the links of the chain.

# Interlaced bracelet

Materials for a 17cm (6¾in) bracelet: 6 × floral print cord, 17cm (6¾in) in length; 9 openwork metal beads with large holes; 1 snap clasp; 2 large ribbon clamps; 2 jump rings

**1** Insert the end of each of the six pieces of cord into a large ribbon clamp. The cords should be perfectly aligned and the same wa. up (with the seam of the cord underneath).

**2** Thread pieces 1 and 2 together on to a bead (piec 1 on top), and position the bead 4.5cm (1¾in) belc the ribbon clamp. Thread pieces 5 and 6 into a secon. bead (piece 6 on top), and position it in line with the first bead.

**3** Thread pieces 2 and 3 on to a bead (piece 2 top), and position the bead 6cm (2½in) below the ribbon clamp. Thread another bead on to pieces 4 and 5 (piece 5 on top), and position it in the same place.

**4** Thread a bead on to pieces 3 and 4 and positior the bead 7.5cm (3in) from the ribbon clamp.

**5** Repeat step 3 and position the beads 9cm (3½in) from the ribbon clamp.

**6** Repeat step 2 and position the beads 10.5cm (4in) from the ribbon clamp.

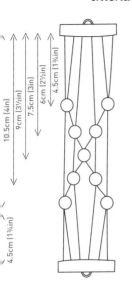

**7** Approximately 4.5cm (1¾in) from the last beads, cut the six pieces of cord off at the same length. Insert the free end of each of the six pieces into the second ribbon clamp. The pieces must be perfectly aligned, exactly as for the first ribbon clamp.

**8** Attach one half of the clasp to each of the ribbon clamps using a jump ring.

**Tip:** By always placing the outermost pieces of cord on top when you are threading the beads, you push the beads downwards, emphasising the fabric pattern more. Alternatively, by putting the innermost pieces of cord on top, you make the beads stand out more on the bracelet.

# Brooches

Materials for a safety pin brooch: 8cm (3¼in) of floral print bias binding; 12cm (4¾in) of floral print cord; 1 safety pin (6cm (2½in)); 1.5cm (½in) of fine trace chain; 2cm (¾in) of snake chain; 1 flat disc with eye hole; 1 coloured star charm matching the bias binding; 2 beads matching the bias binding; 4 jump rings; 1 small cord end; 1 crimp bead

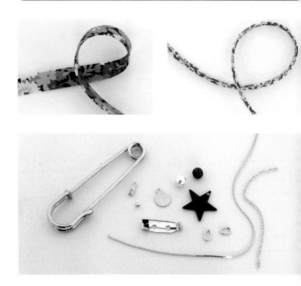

## Making a safety pin brooch:

**1** Make a bow with the cord
(see step 1, page 56).

**2** Stick the bow on to the flat disc, leaving the eye
hole just slightly visible above the bow.
Attach the loop of the disc to the safety pin (on the
non-movable arm) using a jump ring.

**3** Attach the star to the fine trace chain using a
jump ring, then attach the free end of the chain
to the safety pin using a jump ring.

4 Insert one end of the snake chain into the cord
end. Thread the two beads on to the snake
chain, then thread on a crimp bead and crimp it
using flat-nosed pliers at the free end of the chain.
Attach the cord end to the safety pin using a
jump ring.

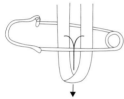

5 Fold the bias binding in half, forming
a loop, then thread the loop down
through the safety pin. Bring the two end
pieces of bias binding round the lower
arm of the safety pin and through the
loop in the binding to form a knot. Pull
firmly on the two pieces to tighten.
Adjust and cut off any excess binding.
Put a spot of light glue inside the bias
binding so that it doesn't come undone
but still remains flexible.

## Making a bow brooch

Materials for a bow brooch: 20cm (7¾in) of bias binding; 1 brooch mount

 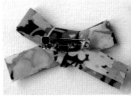

**1** Make a bow with the bias binding, following steps A, B, C and D opposite. Adjust the bow and cut off any excess bias binding. Put a dab of light glue inside the bow so it doesn't come undone but still remains flexible.

**Tip:** Add charms to the brooch by attaching jump rings to the holes in the brooch mount.

**2** Stick the bow on to the brooch mount – not too high up to make sure the bow doesn't flop forwards when you are wearing it.

A

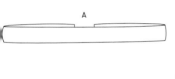

B

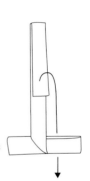

C

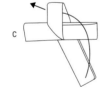

D

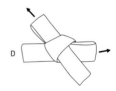

# Magnifying bead jewellery

**Materials for a 17cm (6¾in) bracelet:** a few centimetres (inches) of floral print bias binding; 2 × fine trace chain, 5cm (2in) in length; 1 oval cabochon mount with retaining grips, 20 × 27mm (¾ to 1in); 1 glass oval cabochon; 1 snap clasp; 2 flat discs with eye holes; 4 jump rings

**Materials for the ring:** a few centimetres (inches) of bias binding; 1 ring blank with flat pad, 12mm (½in) in diameter; 1 oval cabochon mount with retaining grips, 14 × 19mm (½ x ¾in); 1 magnifying oval cabochon

## Making the bracelet

**1** Unfold the bias binding and place the cabochon mount on top. Draw round the mount and cut out the fabric following your trace line.

**2** Stick the piece of fabric inside the cabochon mount before placing the cabochon on top. Clos the retaining grips over the cabochon using flat-nosed pliers.

**3** Stick the two flat discs with eye holes on the back of the cabochon mount, one at each end, leaving the eye holes sticking out slightly from under the mount.

**4** Attach a 5cm (2in) length of chain to each of the loops using a jump ring.

**5** Attach one half of the clasp to the free end of eac of the pieces of chain using a jump ring.

## Making the ring

Unfold the bias binding and place the cabochon mount on top. Draw round the mount and cut out the fabric following your trace line.

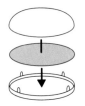

2 Stick the piece of fabric inside the cabochon mount before placing the cabochon on top. Close the retaining grips over the cabochon using flat-nosed pliers.

3 Glue the cabochon mount on to the ring mount.

First published in Great Britian in 2015 by
Search Press Ltd.
Wellwood, North Farm Road,
Tunbridge Wells,
Kent, TN2 3DR

© Larousse 2014
© Dessain et Tolra / Larousse 2012
Original French title published as *Bijoux en Liberty*

English translation by Burravoe Translation Services

Typesetting by Greengate Publishing Services, Tonbridge, Kent

ISBN: 978-1-78221-241-6

Illustrations: Violette Bénilan
Photographs: Ayumi Shino
Hair and Make-up: Manami Kishimoto

Acknowledgements:
The publisher would like to thank Stragier who provided all the bias binding and
piping used for the creations in this book.
http://tissusliberty.blogspot.com
http://stragier.blogspot.com

Printed in China